@RosenTeenTalk

Life Skills

FINANCES IRL

Elissa Bongiorno

ROSEN PUBLISHING

Published in 2025 by The Rosen Publishing Group, Inc.
2544 Clinton Street, Buffalo, NY 14224

First Edition

Editor: Greg Roza
Designer: Rachel Rising

Photo Credits: Cover, pp. 1, 3, 5, 17, 45 Krakenimages.com/Shutterstock.com;Cover Cosmic_Design/Shutterstock.com; Cover, pp. 6, 8, 10, 12 14, 16, 20, 22, 24, 26, 28, 32, 34, 36, 38, 40, 42 Vitya_M/Shutterstock.com; pp. 3, 15 Vector Tradition/Shutterstock.com; pp. 3, 25, Travelpixs/Shutterstock.com; pp. 3, 37 Phongphan/Shutterstock.com; p. 7 svetabelaya/Shutterstock.com; p. 8 Sanit Fuangnakhon/Shutterstock.com; p. 9 BAZA Production/Shutterstock.com; p. 10 Hyejin Kang/Shutterstock.com; p. 11 Andrey_Popov/Shutterstock.com; p. 13 ADragan/Shutterstock.com; p. 16 Pixel-Shot/Shutterstock.com; p. 19 Monkey Business Images/Shutterstock.com; p. 20 MIKHAIL GRACHIKOV/Shutterstock.com; p. 21 Mironov Konstantin/Shutterstock.com; p. 23 Sutthiphong Chandaeng/Shutterstock.com; p. 26 Irina Strelnikova/Shutterstock.com; p. 27 Andrii Zastrozhnov/Shutterstock.com; p. 29 ozrimoz/Shutterstock.com; p. 31 Nattakorn_Maneerat/Shutterstock.com; p. 32 Tanya Antusenok/Shutterstock.com; p. 33 Golubovy/Shutterstock.com; pp. 34, 43 Rawpixel.com/Shutterstock.com; p. 35 SpeedKingz/Shutterstock.com; p. 36 sebra/Shutterstock.com; p. 38 Irina Strelnikova/Shutterstock.com; p. 39 LALAKA/Shutterstock.com; p. 41 karamysh/Shutterstock.com; p. 42 Alina. Alina/Shutterstock.com.

Some of the images in this book illustrate individuals who are models. The depictions do not imply actual situations or events.

Library of Congress Cataloging-in-Publication Data

Names: Bongiorno, Elissa, author.
Title: Finances IRL / Elissa Bongiorno.
Other titles: Finances in real life
Description: [Buffalo] : Rosen Publishing, [2025] | Series: @RosenTeenTalk: life skills | Includes index.
Identifiers: LCCN 2024005910 (print) | LCCN 2024005911 (ebook) | ISBN 9781499477481 (library binding) | ISBN 9781499477474 (paperback) | ISBN 9781499477498 (ebook)
Subjects: LCSH: Finance, Personal--Juvenile literature. | Financial literacy--Juvenile literature.
Classification: LCC HG179.B5826 2025 (print) | LCC HG179.B5826 2025 (ebook) | DDC 332.024--dc23/eng/20240308
LC record available at https://lccn.loc.gov/2024005910
LC ebook record available at https://lccn.loc.gov/2024005911

Manufactured in the United States of America

CPSIA Compliance Information: Batch #CSRYA25. For Further Information contact Rosen Publishing at 1-800-237-9932.

CONTENTS

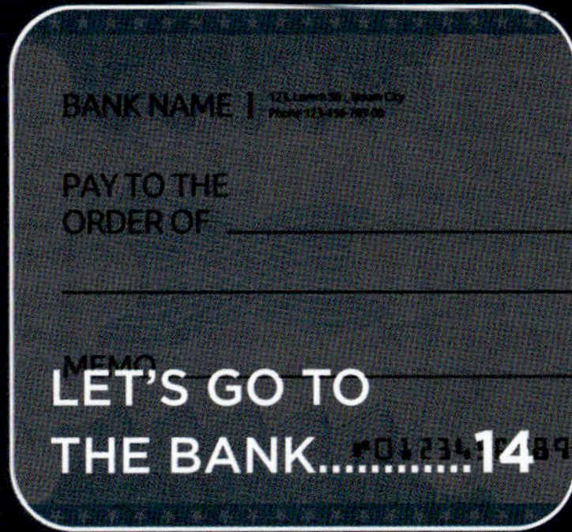

Chapter 1

I Want It Now!

I stomped up the stairs and slammed the door. *My parents are so annoying*! They won't let me get a new phone. My old one broke. How am I supposed to talk to my friends? They said that I need to learn to be *financially literate*. They want me to pay for the phone myself. How am I supposed to do that? I'm a kid!

I counted all the money I had: $23.71. *Not enough*. I needed a job. And a credit card. And a bank account! My parents were right. I had to earn money ASAP. Phones are expensive.

I took a deep breath. Time to go downstairs and talk. Maybe they would drive me to the bank. I could **deposit** my $23.71. Got to start somewhere!

Learning how to manage money is an important life skill. By being responsible with your money, you can accomplish a lot. Saving toward a goal is a great feeling. Give it a try!

WHAT ARE YOUR GOALS?

Think about your future. What do you see? A beach house? A sports car? These are your dreams. They can also be called goals. And you can financially plan for them. How?

It starts with small steps.

1. Define your goal. Be specific. What is it you want?
2. Be realistic. At first, try picking a small goal. This will be easier to accomplish.
3. Set a timeline. When do you want to achieve this goal?
4. Take small steps toward your goal. Begin saving a small amount each week or month. It will add up!

Once you set your goals and begin saving, check in on your progress every month. This way you will know how you are doing. You can track your progress.

By breaking your goals into smaller pieces, you can do more. Want to go on a trip with your friends next year? Save for a plane ticket. Then the hotel. Then food and experiences. Soon, you'll be on your way!

SHORT-TERM GOALS VS. LONG-TERM GOALS

Some goals can be reached by saving for a few months. Some goals take years! Here are some examples of short- and long-term goals. What are your goals?

Short Term	Long Term
phone	car
sneakers	college
designer purse	first apartment
smartwatch	first pet

HOW TO MAKE MONEY

So...you need money! But how do you get it? The U.S. government says you can begin working at 14. Before then, you can talk with your parents about getting an **allowance**. Do chores around the house. If you like kids, consider babysitting.

When looking for a job, think of what you like to do and how much time you have. Are your afternoons and weekends busy with activities? A summer job may be a better fit. A job is a big responsibility.

Babysitting can be a great way to make money. Start by taking a first aid class, so you can be sure to handle **emergencies**. Then ask around your neighborhood. You never know who needs help!

YOUR FIRST PAYCHECK

Once you begin working, you will begin to get a paycheck. This contains the money you have earned. You might get a paper check. Or the money may be deposited directly into your bank account for you.

There will be several numbers on your paycheck. Gross pay is the total amount of money you have earned. But you do not get all that money. Taxes will be taken from your money before you receive it. The money left is called net pay. That is all yours!

On your paycheck, you will see that FICA has been deducted. This stands for Federal Insurance Contributions Act. These funds pay for elderly people and those who need medical care. You might know someone who uses this money, such as a grandparent.

WHAT ARE TAXES, ANYWAY?

Taxes are a percentage of money taken by the government. This money is used to:

- pave roads
- run public schools
- fund fire departments
- fund police departments
- perform medical research
- run public transportation

Taxes are used to help all levels of the government: federal, state, and local. We all contribute. These small amounts add up to help our country run.

BUDGET, BUDGET, BUDGET

Once you start making money, you need a budget. How do you start?

1. Write down how much money you earn each month.
2. Make a list of all the things you spend money on.
3. List how much these items cost and add it up.
4. Subtract that amount from the money you earn.

Now you have a sense of your expenses and **income**. Consider your goals. Do you have money left over each month to save for them? Maybe you'll have to cut back on other items.

Wants vs. Needs

Consider what you *need*. You need breakfast every day. Now think about what you *want*. You want a new pair of shoes, but the ones you have now still fit.

Take the time to make a budget. Be mindful of your expenses. Knowing where you spend your money is power. By setting aside savings each month, you'll be amazed at how your money grows!

THE 50/30/20 RULE

A good way to make a budget is to use the 50/30/20 rule.

- 50 percent: required expenses (bus pass, work uniform, school supplies)
- 30 percent: wants (eating out, gifts for friends)
- 20 percent: savings (future goals)

Chapter 2

LET'S GO TO THE BANK

When you're ready to start saving money, it's time to open a bank account. If you are under 18, you'll need to bring:

- an adult
- the adult's identification
- the adult's account number at the bank
- your **Social Security** card or birth **certificate**
- your first deposit

Make sure to find an account with low or no fees. Once in the bank, your money will earn **interest**. This is a small percentage of money the bank pays you for keeping your money there.

What Type of Account?

Savings account: You can save for your goals. These often have a higher interest rate.

Checking account: You can easily deposit and withdraw money. You will get checks and a debit card to use.

When you want to withdraw money, you can write a check. On the "PAY TO THE ORDER OF" line, write who the money is for. On the line below, write out the amount, like "One hundred dollars." The amount in numerals goes in the box to the right. Then sign your name and date it.

BANKING FEES

Ask your bank about fees when opening your account. Banks can charge you fees for lots of things, including ATM **withdrawals** and monthly **maintenance** fees. Teen accounts may receive special deals.

DEBIT VS. CREDIT

Many people use cards to pay for purchases. But there is a big difference between a debit card and a credit card.

Debit Card: A debit card is linked to your checking account. When you purchase something, the payment comes from the money you deposited.

Credit Card: A credit card loans you the money to make a purchase. You must pay the money back. If you don't pay the money back in one month, you must pay interest. It adds up!

Be mindful of credit card interest rates. Most credit cards charge around 22 percent interest each month. That means if you have a bill for $100 that you do not pay off, the next month you owe $122!

Three Steps to Getting a Credit Card

1. If you're under 18, bring an adult.
2. Shop for a good interest rate.
3. Talk with a grown-up about what you will charge.

You will get a statement each month listing your charges. Carefully go through the items. Make sure you made each purchase. This also helps you understand if you are staying on budget.

My First Account

I had butterflies in my stomach as we walked up to the glass doors. I was opening my first bank account! My mom said that because I was starting my job soon, I needed to get my finances set up. I wanted to go alone, but Mom needed to sign some forms for me, since I'm 16.

I signed my name a bunch of times and filled out some forms. The man at the bank gave me my account number and the bank's **routing number**. He said I could give those to the ice cream store I'm working at. They will set up direct deposit. My paycheck will go right into my account. They'll mail me checks and a debit card. I can't wait to start depositing money!

It's important to talk to your family about money. They can help you open an account. Together, you can work on a plan for your future. It feels great to save.

AN IMPORTANT TEST: YOUR CREDIT SCORE

Your credit score is an important number. It tells banks, credit card companies, phone companies, and more if you are a good financial risk. These companies want to know if you will make your payments on time. Your score will affect renting an apartment and buying a car and house.

The longer you have a credit card, the longer your credit history. This will help your credit score. Be sure to make your payments on time. Keep your **balance** low.

About 55 percent of Americans never check their credit score. You can find your score for free. Your credit card company or a service can help.

A high credit score is 670 and above. A poor to fair score is 300 to 669. There are many ways to improve your score. Make payments on time. Lower your debt. Over time, your score will improve.

CALCULATING YOUR CREDIT SCORE

Here are some things that go into your credit score:

- Bill payment history: Do you pay your bills on time?
- Length of credit history: How long have you had a credit card?
- Amount of credit available: How much can you charge on your credit card? How much of a balance do you carry each month?

INTEREST RATES: SMALL NUMBER, BIG IMPACT

An interest rate is the cost of borrowing money. It is a percentage. Banks and credit card companies charge you when they lend you funds. Remember your credit card balance? You have to pay interest on that amount each month. When you buy a house or car, you will probably borrow money from the bank. You'll have to pay interest on that money. The higher the interest rate, the more you will have to pay each month.

You can also earn interest on the money in your savings account. You are loaning the bank money. They pay you!

Annual percentage rate is another important number. It is the total amount of interest you will pay in one year, plus fees.

The Federal Reserve, a government agency, sets interest rates. Companies then adjust, or change, their rates for consumers, or customers. The number can change often.

Your interest rate depends on your credit score. The higher your score, the lower your interest rate. Make payments on time. Keep your debt down. You'll be an interest rate winner!

CRUNCH THOSE NUMBERS

price of car: $20,000

interest rate: 7 percent

monthly payment for a 36-month loan: $594

total interest paid: $1,400

total price of car with interest: $21,400

Chapter 3

AFTER HIGH SCHOOL

After high school, you've got lots of options, or choices. You might want to go to community college, or to a four-year university. Both cost different amounts of money. They meet different needs.

Community College: You can earn a two-year degree (an associate's degree). Technical certificates are also often available. These can lead you to jobs like EMT, nurse, or bookkeeper.

Four-Year University: You can earn a four-year degree (bachelor's degree). Pick your school wisely. Many study options will be available. Business. Economics. Biology. English. These jobs may lead you to earn more eventually.

Talking Tuition

Talk with your family about costs. It might feel awkward. But it is good to know if they have saved money for your schooling. You can plan together. Set goals that will work for you.

A great way to research colleges is to check out College Navigator. It is run by the National Center for Education Statistics. You can search schools by location, major, and more.

nces.ed.gov/collegenavigator

COST OF TUITION

2022 – 2033 Full-time Student	Tuition per Year
average cost for a public two-year college	**$3,860**
average cost for public four-year college	**$10,940**

529 PLANS

Saving for college is a big task. One tool to help you achieve this goal is a 529 plan. This is a special kind of savings account for education. There are tax benefits. These help when **investing** the money in the account. They also help when taking it out.

Some states have 529 plans. If you live in such a state, you can open an account that way. Family members, including grandparents, can contribute to the account too. Small deposits can build up over time.

Funds in a 529 plan can be used to pay for two- or four-year schools. You can also transfer, or send, account money to a family member, in case you do not use all the money.

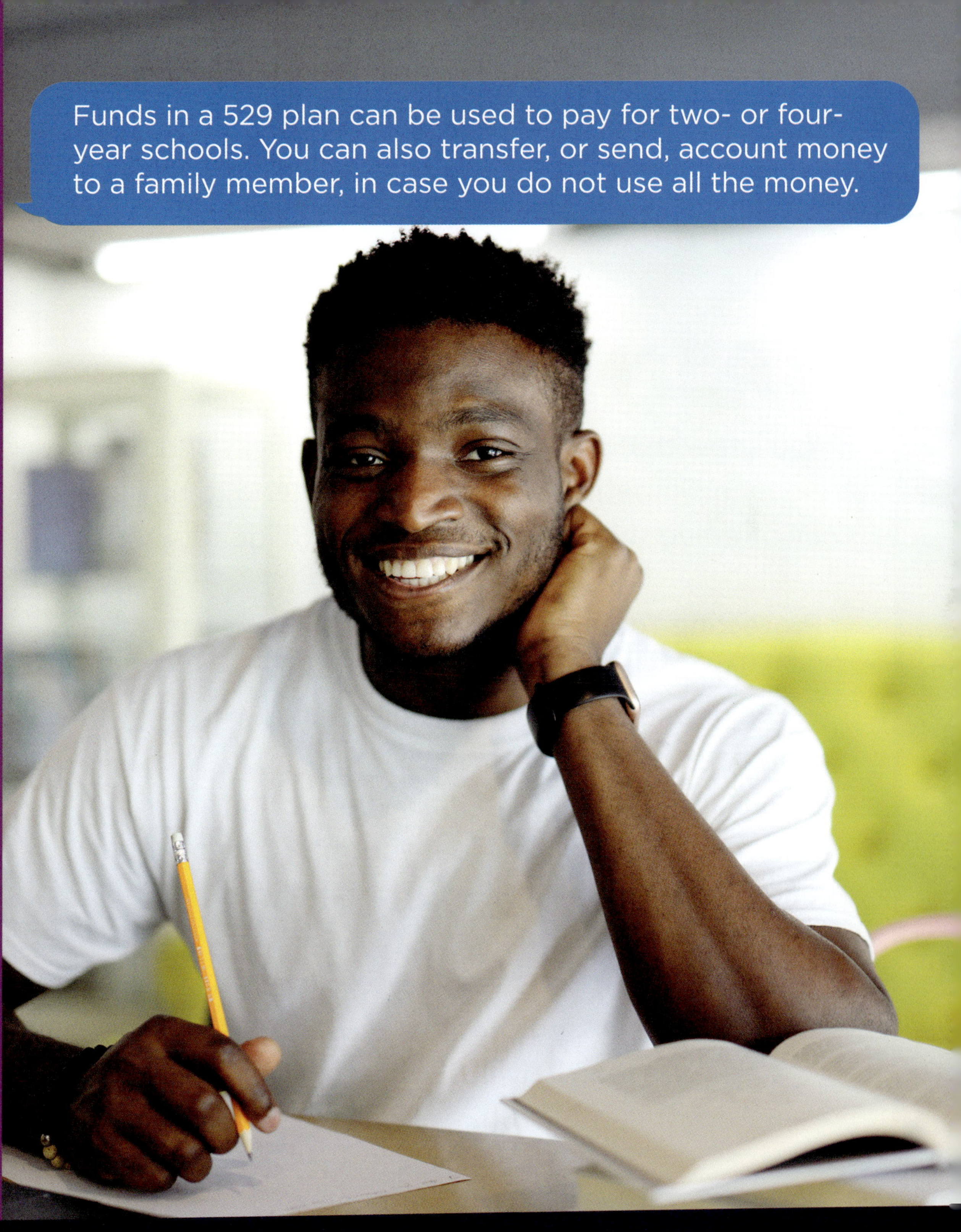

IDENTITY THEFT

You know that not everyone is who they say they are online. Sometimes, people can pretend to be you! They often do this to steal. This is called identity theft.

Protecting Yourself

1. Never give your credit card number over the phone in public. You don't know who is listening.
2. Be careful what email links you click on. You can get a fake email from your bank. If you input your info, people can steal it—and your money. This is called phishing.
3. Shred your mail. Watch out for paper mail with financial information or offers. Make sure you shred it. Make it unreadable before putting it in the trash.

How to Know If Something Is Wrong

1. Keep track of all your charges and withdrawals.
2. Check your accounts often to make sure there are no charges you did not make.
3. Check your credit score. Identity theft will affect your score.

Fast Fact

Nearly 1 million children were victims of identity theft in 2022.

Using complex passwords can help keep your identity safe. Pick a password with at least 15 characters. Don't use any personal details like your name or birthday. These are easy to guess.

The Overdraft

I tapped my card at the coffee shop. My friends were behind me. A red button beeped. The cashier frowned at me.

"Sorry, hon. Your card was declined."

I felt heat creep up my neck. "I just got paid!" I told her. She shrugged.

My friend Javi offered to pay. I pushed him away. I needed to get home to see what was up. I knew not to log on to my banking app here. The Wi-Fi was public, which meant someone could get into my account.

I went home and told my mom. I knew she might be mad. But I needed her help. She told me I'd overdrawn my account. The bank had taken out an overdraft fee of $35. I hadn't kept close enough track of my spending. My mom helped me set up a spreadsheet. I was going to be more careful from now on.

Keep careful track of how much you have earned, and how much you have spent. You'll learn more about your spending habits. Then you can make changes to reach your goals.

BUYER BEWARE

Many people fall for online **scams**, and the scams are getting trickier. Do not give anyone your address or account info without checking with an adult first. An internet search may also tell you if someone is trying to scam you.

Online Contest: A pretend influencer will say you won. They'll ask for your personal info, but you will not get a prize.

Shopping Scam: You might try to buy an item from a fake site. This often happens in video games.

Quizzes: Don't type in details like your address or name.

The Federal Trade Commission is a government agency that helps protect consumers. You can learn more about scams and how to avoid them here: **consumer.ftc.gov/scams**

A recent study found that teens lost $210 million dollars to online scams in 2022. The amount of money lost has increased 2,500 percent since 2017! By being mindful of who you give information to online, you can protect yourself from scams.

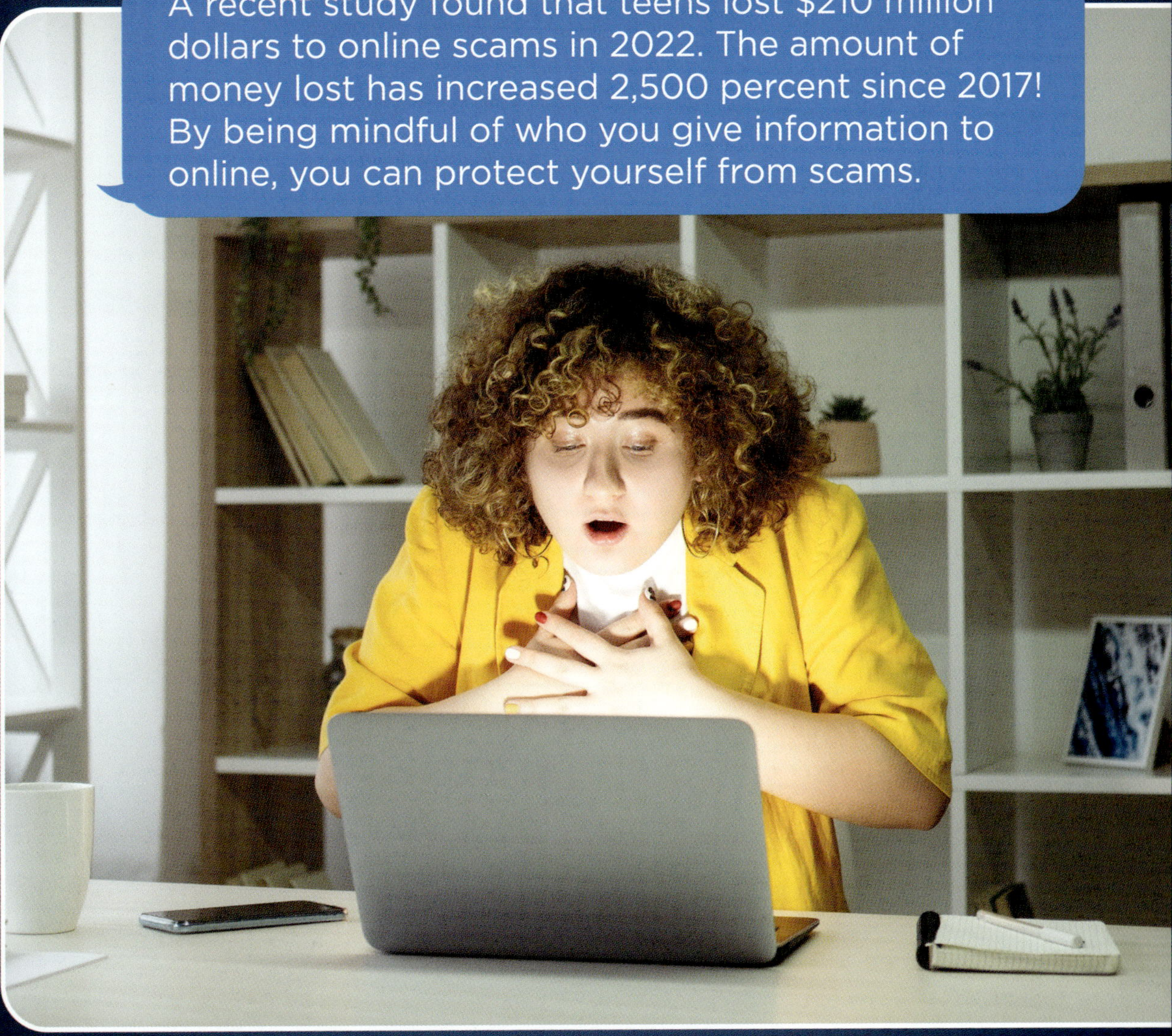

SO, YOU WANT WHEELS

One of your long-term goals may be to have a car. In most states, you cannot get a car loan until you are 18. This means you'll need an adult's help. Talk with your family. Decide together if you want to:

Lease: Renting a new car for a set amount of time, usually two or three years.
Buy: Buying a new or used car, usually with a loan.

Fast Fact

You are legally required to have car **insurance** if you are driving a car. Yearly car insurance costs for teens can range from $1,400 to $4,000. Consider this cost when looking for a car.

As a teen, you can be added to your parent's car insurance. This can help with the cost of the policy. You could save up to $1,000. On your own, teen car insurance can cost more than $5,000 per year.

CAR COSTS

In addition to car payments and insurance, other costs are involved with having a vehicle:

Gasoline: Prices depend on where you live and how much you drive. On average, Americans spend $5,000 a year on gas.

Maintenance: Cars need to be cared for. You'll need to budget for oil changes, tire rotations, and a yearly **inspection**. This can cost up to $1400 a year.

Chapter 4

THINKING AHEAD

You may have heard adults talking about the **stock market**. Investing money is not just for grown-ups. You can try too.

Kids have an advantage over adults: time. Generally, the longer your money is in the stock market, the more profit you will make. Imagine you invested $1,000 in the stock market when you were 10. By the time you were 80, it could be worth $760,000. This assumes the stock market behaves as it always has. There is always risk in investing.

How to Invest

1. Decide on a time frame. It's a good idea to keep your money in for around five to 10 years at least.
2. Do you like taking risks? Or do you prefer to be safe? This will affect which stocks you invest in.
3. Decide on a type of stock. There are many categories to choose from.
4. Talk with an adult. Your parents might have a financial advisor who can help too.

If you'd like to check out investments or investors, go to: **www.investor.gov.** This website, run by a U.S. government agency, can provide lots of information on safe places to invest.

MUTUAL FUNDS FUN

Want to begin investing? Consider a mutual fund. "Mutual" means "shared in common." A mutual fund combines different types of investments. This includes stocks and **bonds**. An advisor watches the fund. Many people invest. This takes away some risk. This is because you are participating in many different types of investments. And so are many other people.

Mutual funds help with an important rule of investing: diversification. This means that your money is invested in different areas. You face a smaller amount of risk.

There are different types of mutual funds. They offer different risks and rewards. One type to consider is a target date fund. It shifts to less risky investments over time. This can be great for college savings.

WHAT'S A MORTGAGE?

Ever thought about where you want to live? In a sky-high apartment? Or maybe near a beach? Do you have this dream? Then it's a good idea to learn about mortgages.

These long-term loans are often for 15 or 30 years. Many people save up a down payment to give the bank. This will make their monthly payment less. This is because they are borrowing less money. Often a down payment is 20 percent of the total home price. Many mortgage options are available.

What makes up a mortgage payment? It's more than just the total you owe the bank.

principal: This amount is applied to the total you owe the bank.

insurance and taxes: Often homeowners must have insurance. And don't forget about property and school taxes!

interest: The bank charges interest on its loan.

Budget for your monthly payment. This will help when house shopping. Remember to save for house repairs and maintenance too.

If you do not have 20 percent for a down payment, you can pay mortgage insurance. This is an additional fee added to your monthly payment. It assures the bank payments will still be made if you cannot pay.

WHAT'S RETIREMENT?

It may be hard to believe, but one day you'll be ready to retire. Retirement is like other investments. The more time you have to save, the better. Here are two common options:

- **Employee Programs:** Some jobs offer retirement investment plans. These are often called 401(k)s. It is a great idea to invest in these programs. Sometimes your employer will contribute, or give money, to this account too.
- **Individual Retirement Fund (IRA):** These accounts can help with taxes, now and when you retire.

Investment Tip

Auto-deposit is a great way to save. Select an amount you can save each month. Then have it automatically deposited in your savings account. The money will add up.

Fast Fact

The average American will be retired for 20 years. Start saving early. Every bit helps.

Nearly 77 percent of Americans are saving for retirement. When you start earning money, join them! You'll be glad that you did.

BEWARE!

You might get tempted to withdraw money from your retirement account. But watch out! If you do, you may have to pay big **penalties**. You can lose money for now and for later. Try your best not to touch the account.

Chapter 5

Financially Literate!

I bounced from foot to foot as I waited in line at the bank. I was depositing my latest paycheck. I couldn't wait for the receipt. It was going to show me my new balance.

I'd been super good about my spending. My parents helped me set up a spreadsheet budget. I type in everything I earn. And everything I spend. Seeing all those numbers really helps me. Now I know I didn't need that second latte at the mall. A small coffee worked for me. Because I still had my eyes on the prize. My phone.

I smiled when I saw my balance. I was just three more paychecks away. In six weeks, that new phone would be mine. And even better: I earned it.

Want to start tracking expenses? Check out the Junior Achievement Budgeting and Income Worksheets. They have templates to get you started. Soon, you'll be financially literate too.

jausa.ja.org/programs/supplements/ja-teen-budgeting-income-and-spending-worksheets

GLOSSARY

allowance: Money that a parent or guardian regularly gives to a child, sometimes earned by doing chores or work.

balance: The amount of money in a bank account, or the money owed on a credit card.

bond: A signed paper promising payment of a certain sum on or before a stated day and issued by a government or corporation as proof of money owed.

certificate: A document that is proof of some fact.

deposit: To put money into a bank account.

emergency: An unexpected situation that needs quick action.

income: Money earned at a job.

inspection: A yearly checkup on a car by a mechanic.

insurance: A contract by which someone guarantees for a fee to pay someone else for the value of property if it is lost or damaged, or to pay a specified amount for injury or death.

interest: A charge for borrowed money that is generally a percentage of the amount borrowed.

invest: To put money into something with the hope of getting more money back.

maintenance: The upkeep of property or tools.

penalty: Punishment, such as an extra fee, for not meeting certain conditions.

routing number: A number banks use to help move money from one account or person to another.

scam: To fool someone to get something from them.

Social Security: A U.S. government program established in 1935 to include old-age and survivors insurance, contributions to state unemployment insurance, and old-age assistance.

stock market: A market for buying and selling stocks, which represent partial ownership of a company or business.

withdrawal: Money taken out of a bank account.

INDEX